# boyzone
## in person

# boyzone
## in person

**Eddie Rowley**

**The official book produced with the exclusive co-operation of the band**

First published in Great Britain in 1996
by Virgin Books
an imprint of Virgin Publishing Limited
332 Ladbroke Grove
London W10 5AH

© 1996 Boyzone. Under licence to Underworld.
Licensed by Copyright Promotions Limited.

Photographs supplied by Idols Licensing & Publicity Ltd.

The right of Eddie Rowley to be identified as the author of this work
has been asserted by him in accordance with the Copyright, Designs and
Patents Act 1988

A catalogue record for this book is available from the British Library.

ISBN 1 85227 656 8

Printed in Great Britain

Designed by Slatter~Anderson
For Virgin Publishing: Philip Dodd

It seemed like an impossible dream. Growing up, we all fantasised about becoming pop stars. Everyone does, especially when you see your idols on the TV or hear them on the radio. They inspire you.

You dream about fame, but you never really expect it to become reality. In our case, the opportunity to go for it came our way. And we grabbed it.

Now we're pop stars. We're performing on all the pop shows. We're appearing in all the teen magazines. And it still feels like a dream.

We didn't know at the start just how big a challenge we were taking on. And just as well, too, because we mightn't have had the courage to go all the way.

We're glad we did. It's been hard work - and still is - but at the end of the day it's a great life. And it's all thanks to you, the fans. Your love and support made our dream come true. Now, in this book, we're revealing our private thoughts and taking you inside the world of Boyzone as we live our dream. We teamed up with our Irish pop writer pal, Eddie Rowley, to give you an honest and revealing account of our amazing lives in the fast lane of pop.

In addition to our own input, we also asked Eddie to tell the story as he sees it. We love the book and hope it gives you lots of pleasure as well.

THE EXAM RESULTS WERE OUT. BUT RONAN KEATING HADN'T A CARE IN THE WORLD. LIKE HIS PALS, RONAN SHOULD HAVE BEEN PACING THE FLOORS, NERVOUSLY NIBBLING AT HIS FINGER NAILS AS HE WAITED FOR NEWS OF HIS ACADEMIC ACHIEVEMENTS. INSTEAD, THE YOUNG HUNK WAS BUSY FENDING OFF ADORING FEMALE FANS OUTSIDE HIS FRONT DOOR... AND LAPPING UP THE ATTENTION.

It was August 1994. Earlier that year, Ronan - then 17 - had dropped out of school to make a bid for stardom with his country's first 'boy' band.

The 'dream boat' knew that major success was on the way. Girls throwing underwear up at his bedroom window was a good sign!

Shane Lynch, who had been working as a trainee mechanic in his dad's garage when he left to join Boyzone, was also waking up every morning to the sound of a chorus of girls chanting his name. Round at the homes of ex-shoe shop attendant Steve Gately, former mechanic Mikey Graham and one-time clothes store assistant Keith Duffy it was the same story.

With the exception of Mikey, the Boyz had been chosen at auditions in Dublin the previous November. There were six members at the start - then two were dropped and Mikey was drafted in. Ireland had never seen anything like it before. The country that spawned rock supergroup U2 had never produced a

successful pop group.

Boyzone got off to a shaky start with a disastrous first TV appearance - and the critics virtually wrote them off.

Irish showbiz impresario Louis Walsh, who managed Eurovision Song Contest winners Johnny Logan and Linda Martin, created Boyzone.

He worked feverishly on their formula for success and refused to be thwarted when record companies closed the door in his face.

Even when his financial resources hit

rock bottom, Louis had the courage to persist with his dream.

He took on a financial backer and co-manager, John Reynolds, who owns a trendy Dublin nighclub called The Pod.

The breakthrough came when record company boss Paul Keogh of Polygram Ireland signed them up.

With a 'dream team' now behind them, Boyzone took Ireland by storm with 'Working My Way Back To You', a single that was never released outside the country.

But to reach dizzy heights, the Boyz still had to conquer the massive UK market. Success there would open up Europe and the rest of the world to them.

It was the '94 Smash Hits Roadshow that introduced Boyzone to British fans - and it ignited a red-hot love affair that has grown and grown.

Boyzone walked away with the Best New Act award at the Smash Hits Poll Winners' party in December '94 and completed a mind-blowing year by reaching No 2 in the British charts that Christmas with 'Love Me For A Reason'.

Boyzone were on a roll. Their debut album, Said And Done, went straight to number one in Britain - even U2 couldn't pull off that feat with their first release.

Bono sent a fax to congratulate the young heroes as they finally hit the super league of pop. But he failed to tell the hot newcomers just how crazy it was going to be.

STEVE GATELY

FIVE GIGGLING GIRLS, ALL ATTIRED IN LIGHT BLUE STAFF UNIFORMS, ARE HOVERING IN THE HOTEL CORRIDOR, WAITING TO WAYLAY STEVE GATELY WHEN HE EMERGES FROM HIS ROOM JUST BEFORE MID-DAY.

**"MY MAIN AMBITION IN LIFE,**

**MY BIGGEST AMBITION, IS TO**

**SING FOR A WALT DISNEY**

**MOVIE. THAT'S WHAT I REALLY,**

**REALLY WANT TO DO."**

Brandishing scraps of paper bearing four scribbles, evidence that the other members of Boyzone have already been nabbed, these young British fans are determined that Steve won't escape the net.

They're slightly apprehensive about approaching Steve because he has the reputation of being the shyest member of the group. But when he finally appears, the young heart-throb accedes to their requests with all the charm and confidence of a true star.

There was a time when Steve only emerged from his shell while performing on stage. Behind the scenes the young artiste was quiet and introverted, sometimes a sad, lonely figure. But once the show started, he would rise to the occasion and blossom into a self-assured, happy-go-lucky pop performer.

While Steve craved stardom, he found the lifestyle difficult to cope with when Boyzone were first thrust into the major league. All the early interviews with Steve would usually refer to the fact that he was 'homesick'.

It's true that Steve missed the emotional support of his family when he first left home, but three years down the road the young entertainer has grown up and come to terms with his new life.

"This year has been a lot easier. I don't let things get to me as much as I used to. I used to worry a lot. I never got to eat or sleep properly. Stuff like that."

Steve, like many his age, was dogged by nagging insecurities. Not least his looks.

These days, however, he feels good about himself.

"Now, I work on my image more. I try not to let things bother me, which is hard to do. I make sure I get my sleep. I take vitamins. I keep myself in good 'nick'. I think that's very, very important and that has really helped me.

"And being in Boyzone has made me

"I'M COPING A LOT

BETTER NOW. AND

ALTHOUGH I STILL LOVE

TO GET HOME, I DON'T

MISS IT AS MUCH AS

I USED TO."

grow up a lot more. It has made me wiser to people and helped me develop as a person.

"I don't think I've changed too much, only for the better. My mother said to me, 'Jeez, you've changed.' And I said, 'In what way?' She said, 'I can't believe how happy you are. You just look so happy now.'

"For a while I lost a lot of confidence. I lost a lot of faith in myself. But now I've got it all together again. I now feel that I deserve whatever I get because whatever I get I work for.

"I'm still not confident in certain situations. But when I'm on stage, I've just got the most amazing confidence. I don't know where it comes from. The feeling I get is just incredible."

You can actually see the metamorphosis happening before your eyes when the lights go up and Steve steps out into the public arena. The quietest member of the group literally glows with happiness and dominates the stage with the confidence of a lion prowling around in the wilderness. Now a young icon and role model for millions of fans, Steve has his own idols. The King Of Pop himself, Michael Jackson, inspired the young Steve to strive for life in the limelight.

Steve's ambition is to have an audience with the

**"I've always wanted to do this. My life is dedicated to this. I wanted to be famous. I wanted to be in the limelight."**

STEVE GATELY

enigmatic Jackson to suss out the real person behind the public persona.

Steve knows that as soon as a star's success begins to fade, so too do the multitude of hangers-on. But there is more to Steve Gately's character than meets the eye. Deep down, he's a very spiritual guy.

record company's office. It's incredible inside. It's a really beautiful place.

"I came across it around the time of the auditions for the group. I went in and sat down and started to pray: 'Please God, help me to get into this band. It's something I really want to do. I love it. I don't know if I'm really

good enough, but I'll try my best.' "God loves a trier. I went in there every night for a week, praying and hoping. It actually relaxed me as well. Afterwards, when I secured my place in the group, I went back to the church to say 'Thanks'. Churches are lovely, peaceful places. I do put my trust in God and I do believe in God." Although the media has linked Steve to a number of female stars, there is no one special in his life.

## "I'd love to meet Michael Jackson to see what he's really like, to actually sit down and have a chat with him. And I'd love to meet Janet Jackson as well."

"I have my religion - I'm a Catholic - and I do pray. Before I got into the band, I remember going to Whitefriars Street in Dublin where there's a beautiful church near our

"RELATIONSHIPS ARE VERY DIFFICULT AT THE MOMENT. IT'S VERY HARD WHEN YOU'RE NEVER IN THE ONE PLACE AT THE ONE TIME. WE'RE ALWAYS IN DIFFERENT COUNTRIES."

"You do meet a lot of people, but I'm just so busy and I've got a lot of things that I want to achieve: you've got to run with the ball when you have it. We have it at the moment, so it'd be mad not to take advantage of the opportunities that are there while we're hot and happening. It's a long life and there'll be plenty of time for relationships in the future. I'll probably wait until the band is nearly over, then I'll say 'Now is the time to get into a relationship'. But it's going to be so hard to find the right person."

Steve has simple needs in life, the most important being the respect of other people. "The way people treat you is so important to me. The way people look at me, the way people talk to me. I don't class myself as a bad person and I would be devastated if other people thought

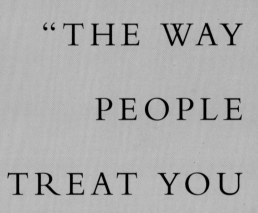

"THE WAY PEOPLE TREAT YOU IS SO IMPORTANT TO ME... I'M A VERY CARING PERSON. I CARE ABOUT EVERYBODY."

"I ALWAYS WANTED TO PUT MY AREA ON THE MAP AND NOW I'VE DONE IT. THERE'S A LOT OF TALENT DOWN MY STREET AND I HOPE THAT WHAT I HAVE ACHIEVED WILL BE AN INSPIRATION TO OTHERS. YOU'VE JUST GOT TO WORK FOR IT. AND I DID WORK FOR IT. I REALLY DID. I WENT TO EVERY AUDITION FOR DIFFERENT THINGS AND I SWEATED IT OUT. I STUDIED ACTING. I STUDIED DANCING. EVERY OPPORTUNITY THAT CAME UP I TRIED FOR IT."

# "I'm a friendly person myself. I'm genuinely friendly

with everyone. But when people are not nice to me, that's a major kick to me."

give me a hug and say: 'Don't worry about it. Things are going to be alright'. And I think, 'Well, I've got four brilliant mates that love me and I love them as well'. It's so important to me. "Of course I worry about it all ending, but I don't think about it that much. I don't get too deep into thinking about it because I get really frightened. I do worry about it now and then because I don't want it to end. Of course, I'd like to do other things as well, but I'm totally enjoying this for the moment.

"I come from a pretty rough area in Dublin. Not a lot of people who come from there get the opportunity that I got. But I really did work for it. Everyone in my locality is really proud of me. They say, 'Fair play to ya'." Steve even had a couple of minor roles as an extra in movies like The Commitments and In The Name Of The Father. His part in the latter, unfortunately, ended up on the floor of the editing suite.

"Nobody pushed me into anything I did. My parents asked, 'What do you want to do?' And when I told them they said, 'Ok, go and do it'.

"I never left Ireland until I got into

differently. I'm a very caring person. I care about everybody. I care about every matter that goes on. I'm a very sensitive person, very emotional. I could never hurt anybody. I couldn't hurt a fly. I'm just not that type of person.

"In the band I get a great kick out of the lads. They keep me happy as well. They look after me. If they see me upset, they always come over and

It's the best thing that has ever happened to me. It has really helped me a lot in my life as well."

Steve emerged from Seville Place in the north inner city of Dublin. It has a strong community spirit, but is battling to overcome the dual problems of drugs and unemployment.

Steve even lost a close friend to drugs, but he has vowed never to experiment with deadly substances himself.

Boyzone. If you'd told me a couple of years ago, 'You're going to go to foreign destinations like Miami', I would have laughed in your face. I could never have imagined in my wildest dreams that I would have achieved so much by the age of 20.

"When it all dies down, I'll sit back and say, 'Look at what I've achieved. Look at what I've done with my life'. I will cry, of course I will. I'll feel very sad about it. But I'll say, 'Well, I've made so many people happy'. And that is such an achievement in itself."

"IF I SEE ONE OF OUR VIDEOS  AND IT'S PRETTY COOL,

THAT GIVES ME A GOOD FEELING.

GOING TO A NEW COUNTRY FOR THE FIRST TIME AND GETTING

A LOVELY WELCOME MAKES ME FEEL GREAT.

BEING ON STAGE IS THE BEST, THOUGH."

THE HOTEL REGISTER SHOWED NO TRACE OF ITS STAR GUESTS. THEY HAD NO MESSRS KEATING, GATELY, LYNCH, GRAHAM OR DUFFY BOOKED IN. "SORRY, THERE IS NO ONE OF THAT NAME STAYING HERE" WAS THE RESPONSE TO PEOPLE TRYING TO TRACK THEM DOWN.

**"AS FAR AS THE FANS ARE CONCERNED, WE COULDN'T HAVE STARTED IN A BETTER PLACE THAN IRELAND."**

Like most stars, Boyzone never check into hotels under their own names in order to avoid the barrage of phone calls that would undoubtedly greet them during their stay.

Instead, Steve can be found under the name of Stephen Jackson. The Jackson obviously taken from his idol, Michael.

Mikey likes to use the pseudonym Michael Corleone, a clue to the type of movie characters that turn him on.

Shane goes by the name of Shane Jetaime, the key to the subject that obviously occupies his thoughts.

Ronan and Keith are Kelly and Morgan respectively. At least, they were. All those names will now be shelved, no doubt, since they're appearing here.

The fans are the life-blood of the group. They're the people who buy their records, albums, videos and books and give the Boyz an incredible lifestyle as a result.

But the fans' access to the individuals in Boyzone has to be carefully controlled to ensure that a semi-normal relationship is maintained between the two parties.

Boyzone are a magnet for girls and it's no secret that they don't live like monks. Keith and Mikey have entered the dadzone and Ronan, Steve and Shane have been linked to several divas of the pop world.

Love and romance, however, plays

second fiddle to Boyzone. The Boyz are adamant that, while they indulge in normal, healthy interaction with the opposite sex, their supergroup takes precedence over their personal lives. Keith reveals: "Obviously there are different relationships going on all the time. The unattached guys meet different girls and fall head over heels in love, but it might only last a couple of weeks. And in that couple of weeks, the person could be hell to talk to. So, we've come to an agreement that it doesn't matter how close you come to somebody, Boyzone comes first.

"We know what we want and we know how to get it and we know how to ruin it as well. We just have to make sure we do the right thing all the time."

There was a time when Shane had no concept of the effect he has on the fans who meet him. To his credit, he never stood back for a moment and thought about his celebrity status. In his own mind, he was simply a normal bloke called Shane Lynch who happened to be lucky enough to hit the big time with a pop group. He often wondered why the fans went weak at the knees and trembled as he put his arms around them for a souvenir photograph. Shane simply couldn't comprehend it. Until he met a group he admired himself.

"I couldn't understand the way the

# "Our **fans** are like our family and friends on the road and we respect them for that."

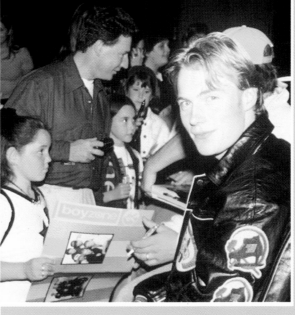

the group from humble beginnings right through their rise into the super league. And the Boyz will always be grateful for their backing. "Our fans are the reason why we're here", says Mikey. "They can't do any wrong in my eyes. And the fans at home in Ireland are our best audience. When we play the Point Depot in Dublin, there's nowhere in the world we get the kind of reaction we enjoy there. They just lift the roof."

The Boyz also love it when they arrive in new countries and find hundreds and often thousands of young girls waiting to welcome them. It's the best feeling in the world, they say.

Keith: "Even though you mightn't get to talk to them, it makes you feel at home straight away. You'd be feeling a little bit homesick if they weren't there."

fans reacted when they met me. As far as I'm concerned I'm normal. Then I met this famous group - I won't say who they are - and the way I felt made me understand how people feel when they meet Boyzone."

Back home in Dublin, there's a hardcore of fans who maintain vigils outside the home of the Boyz when they're back in their native country. They're the people who supported

the signals that this can transmit to their loyal supporters... that they are deliberately snubbing them. But they feel that, in general, the fans understand why they can't always give them time.

Steve: "I say 'Listen girls, I have to go, see you soon.' And they say, 'OK, no problem.' They know that if I have time I'll spend it with them.

"Sometimes girls come round when I've arrived home in Ireland. Some girls come knocking on my door when I may be in the shower and my mum will say 'Oh, he's in the shower, would you like to call back later?' And they say 'Oh, no problem, we'll come back tomorrow.'

"They understand that I've just got in and I need time to organise myself."

Ronan has magical memories of Boyzone's first visit to the Far East. The fact that he was actually getting the opportunity to see that part of the world was exciting in itself, but he was blown away by the reception waiting for him and the Boyz.
He revealed: "We didn't know what to expect. When we arrived in Bangkok there were hundreds of people there to meet us. The army was there. The National Guard. The Chief of Police. Unbelievable. They gave us a traditional welcome by putting flowers around our neck. Then we went out through the main doors and there must have been thousands upon thousands of fans there. We had gone quadruple platinum out there, so it was mad. We went from Bangkok to Japan, Japan to Hong Kong, Hong Kong to Singapore and we were treated like kings wherever we went. It's an

experience to remember for life."
As they race through airports to catch flights, Boyzone are often stopped in their tracks by their army of followers, seeking autographs and photographs with the individual members of the group.
On occasions like that, it's not always possible to hang around and give the fans their time. Boyzone are aware of

KEITH: "I'M VERY GRATEFUL FOR WHAT OUR

FANS HAVE DONE FOR ME AS A PERSON. THEY

HAVE GIVEN ME A WONDERFUL FEELING OF

SELF-WORTH AND THAT'S THE BEST THING YOU

COULD EVER DO FOR ANYBODY."

M I K E Y   G R A H A M

MIKEY GRAHAM EYES UP THE NEWSPAPER HACK, FLASHING HIM A LOOK THAT IS REMINISCENT OF CLINT EASTWOOD'S DIRTY HARRY CHARACTER.

**"I'VE BECOME**

**VERY WISE**

**BECAUSE MY EYES**

**HAVE BEEN OPENED TO AN**

**AWFUL LOT OF THINGS."**

It's another city and another interview. Another guy looking for an 'angle' on Boyzone. And Mikey, as usual, is on his guard. The young star hasn't met this geezer from the press before and, other than flippant answers, he doesn't give anything away.

If there's one thing that Mikey Graham has learned in the last three years with Boyzone, it's to be wary of the strangers who flit in and out of their lives along the way.

He's also intensely private, guarding his personal life with the tenacity of a pit-bull terrier. "I feel that what I do outside of Boyzone is my own business. That's just the type of person I am. I want to keep that end of my life private. Now some might say 'Look here, you choose to be in the public eye, therefore you're public property'. What I say to that is, 'Crap', that's what I say, y'know what I mean.

My private life is my private life and nobody owns me."

Mikey is the oldest member of the group and he also has a background in showbiz. Both Mikey and Shane went to the Billie

Barry stage school in Dublin from an early age and Mikey was there until he was 15. (He tasted stardom as a kid when he appeared in a couple of TV advertisements, one for Mikado biscuits and the other for the ESB, which is the Irish electricity board.) Going into Boyzone, then, he wasn't a star-struck, budding performer who was blissfully ignorant of the pit-falls that many young artists fall prey to. Life in the fast lane of pop music, though, doesn't seem to have left him too disillusioned.
He still gets a kick out of his career, but

approaches the whole scene with a healthy cynicism.

"I take my work seriously, but I don't take the whole scene seriously. I've definitely become more wary of people and I'm glad of that. Initially, it was a bit frightening to realise that it's a tough old world. But I now know that, if I wanted to, I could have the capability to be a right shark myself out there. I've learnt that much."

One night, as the sound of Sean Maguire fills the backstage area, belting out the hit 'Good Day' in the arena, Mikey is tucked away in a corner, chatting quietly on the phone. He's hungry for news about the little lady who is now the centre of his life - his baby daughter. What sounds did she make today? Is she still looking for 'Da Da'?

Looking back on the times I met Mikey when he was still hiding the secret of his girlfriend's pregnancy, I now realise why he was so preoccupied, even aloof. Staying in the background. A troubled guy trying to get to grips with his life which was increasingly becoming more complex.

He now admits there were times when he reached breaking point. "Well, I didn't actually cry, but once or twice it

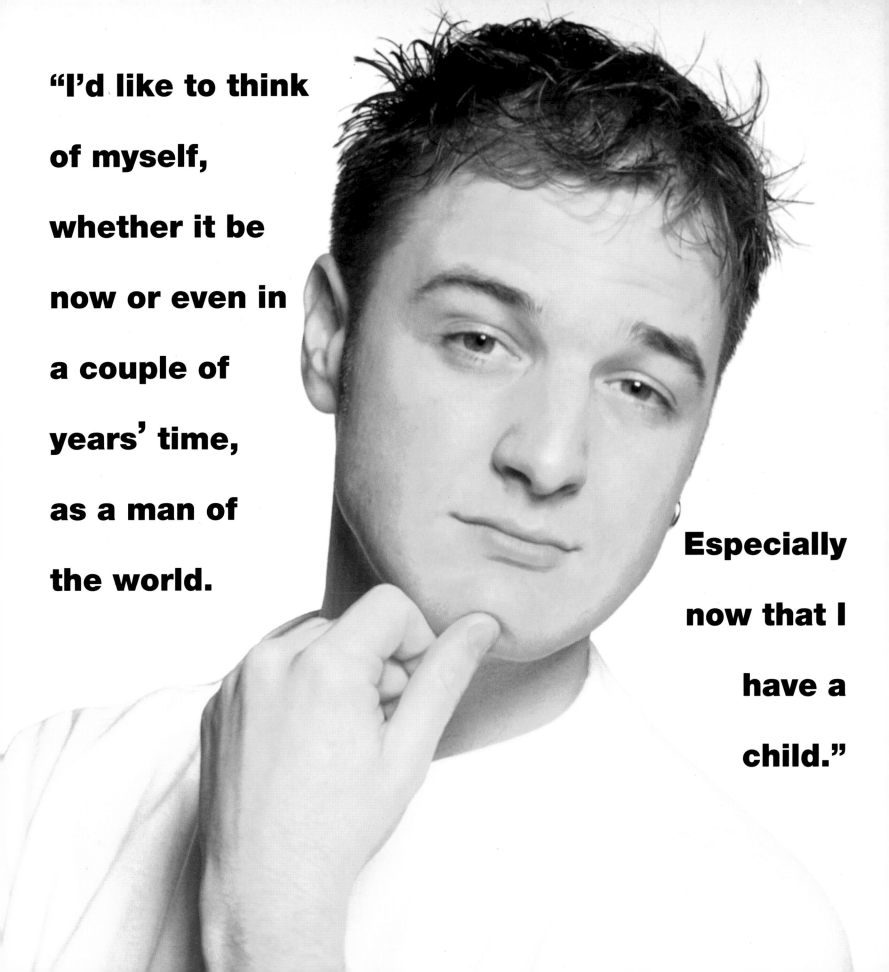

"I'd like to think of myself, whether it be now or even in a couple of years' time, as a man of the world.

Especially now that I have a child."

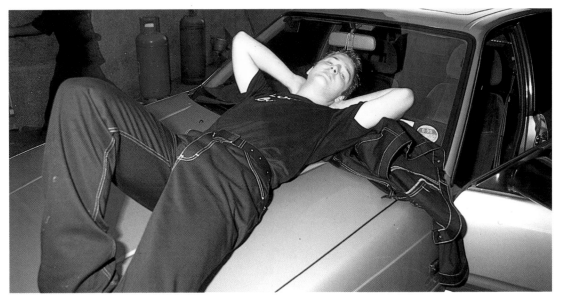

situation and chart a new direction. "I think from the day she was born that's happened. You feel a lot more responsible for a start. You feel like a different person because you're no longer thinking for yourself.

"She's made a huge difference to my life. I wasn't sure what it was all about at the time, but she's made it all worthwhile now."

The lure of Ireland hasn't lost its grip on Mikey and he has set up a

actually got to me, as it did to most of the guys.

"It's OK when you're just dealing with the demands of the group alone, but if you have any pressures in different areas of your life as well, then it can all get on top of you if you're in a fit of confusion about everything happening in your life. I had lots of different things going on, what with the baby on the way and things like that.

"Obviously that's something I had to come to terms with. It was a strange period... pressure... a stressful time. I won't deny that the thought went through my head about leaving the band.

"But you just go through that for a short time and then you calm down and put it all back into perspective. You realise there is no way in the world you'd give this up."

As a dad, Mikey had to re-evaluate his

If there's a hard-nosed businessman in the group, it's Mikey. He's already plotting life after Boyzone. With the responsibilities of parenthood, security is now the key to his life. Discussing business with him, you soon realise that Mikey is going to be a mogul of the future.

# "One of my dreams is to launch my own Hard Rock-type bar restaurant over here in Dublin."

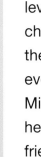

permanent home in his native Dublin. "When I'm at home I hang out with my family and friends. They're the people who keep me level. Unfortunately, I don't get a chance to do too much of that these days. But it'll all calm down eventually."

Mikey is adamant about one thing, he doesn't want to lose the real friends in his life by acting like a prima donna.

I want to keep them in my life.
"I know where it's all at, so I'm going to keep myself on the same level all the time. I just try to treat everybody the same."
"Friends that I hadn't seen since Boyzone all started were a bit apprehensive around me when they met me. But within five minutes around me they realise that I'm still just the plain old Mikey Graham they always knew. It's a weird thing. They forget

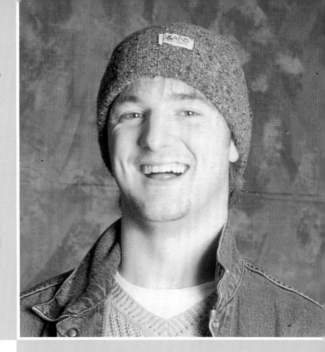

"I don't see the point in changing my attitudes to people or my personality traits just because we're successful and well known. I'll walk down my street and be the same old Mikey that everyone knew before all this happened because the day will come that this will be no more.
"Whether I'm successful or not is immaterial, it's what I feel for other people that's important. And I have a lot of good friends, real friends and

"IRELAND IS

THE BEST

LITTLE PLACE IN

THE WORLD."

about the star bit and that's the same with everyone I meet."
Mikey credits his parents, and the values they instilled in him growing up, for his down to earth attitude. "The qualities that I have, I think, are completely excellent. I've been reared with them. The qualities are just those of a normal person with values, moral values, things I've been brought up with."

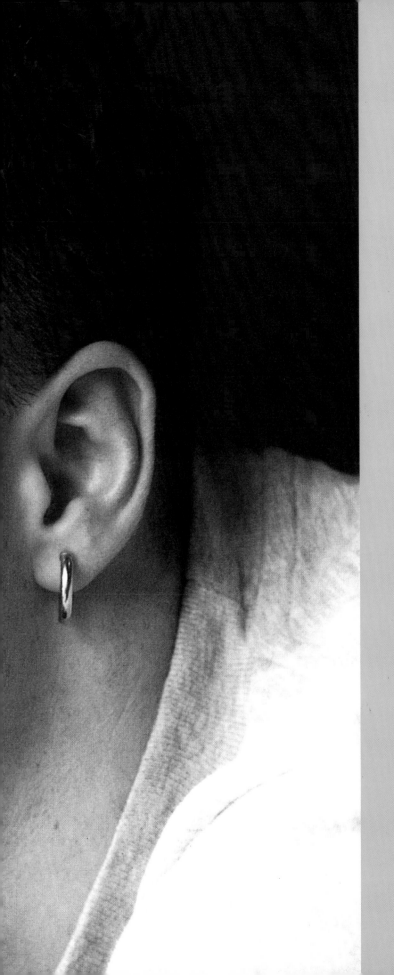

"THE MIKEY GRAHAM YOU SEE BEFORE YOU IS

THE PRODUCT OF A GOOD UPBRINGING. ANY

DECENT ATTRIBUTES I HAVE, I GOT FROM MY

PARENTS AND MY FAMILY AND I'M NOT GOING TO

LOSE THEM OVERNIGHT. I'M NOT GOING TO TURN

INTO SOME SNOBBY LITTLE PIG."

IT'S A CLAMMY
AFTERNOON IN MID-APRIL
AND A GROUP OF ABOUT
TWENTY EXCITED YOUNG
SCHOOLGIRLS ARE PATIENTLY
HANGING AROUND A DOUR
BUILDING IN A GRIM,
INDUSTRIAL DOCKLANDS
AREA ON THE BOUNDARY
OF DUBLIN'S
INNER CITY.

The small army of
dedicated fans are waiting for
their idols, Boyzone, who are
shedding blood, sweat and tears as
they work their way through gruelling
rehearsal routines inside the bleak
looking premises.
Situated on Barrow Street, the grungy
complex houses rehearsal studios
and is known as The Factory. It was
indeed once a factory, but has now
been converted into a facility for
groups to rehearse and record.
The Factory  plays host to the cream
of the world's music talent these

days.  Artists from U2 to David Bowie
and Chris de Burgh have availed
themselves of its facilities as they
geared up for world tours.
Celebrity spotters and autograph
hunters can often be seen hanging
around the building. Their ranks have
swelled with the arrival of the
Boyzone brigade.
During the two weeks that Boyzone
are holed up in their training camp,
top Irish traditional group Clannad
and trad pop family The Corrs are

also busily
honing and shaping their
live shows before setting out
on tour.
The Corrs feature three
stunning sisters, Andrea,
Sharon and Caroline, and they
get on famously with the Boyz.
There's some good-natured
slagging between the two
camps.
Andrea, a classic beauty who
also combines her singing with
a pinch of acting - she has
featured in The Commitments

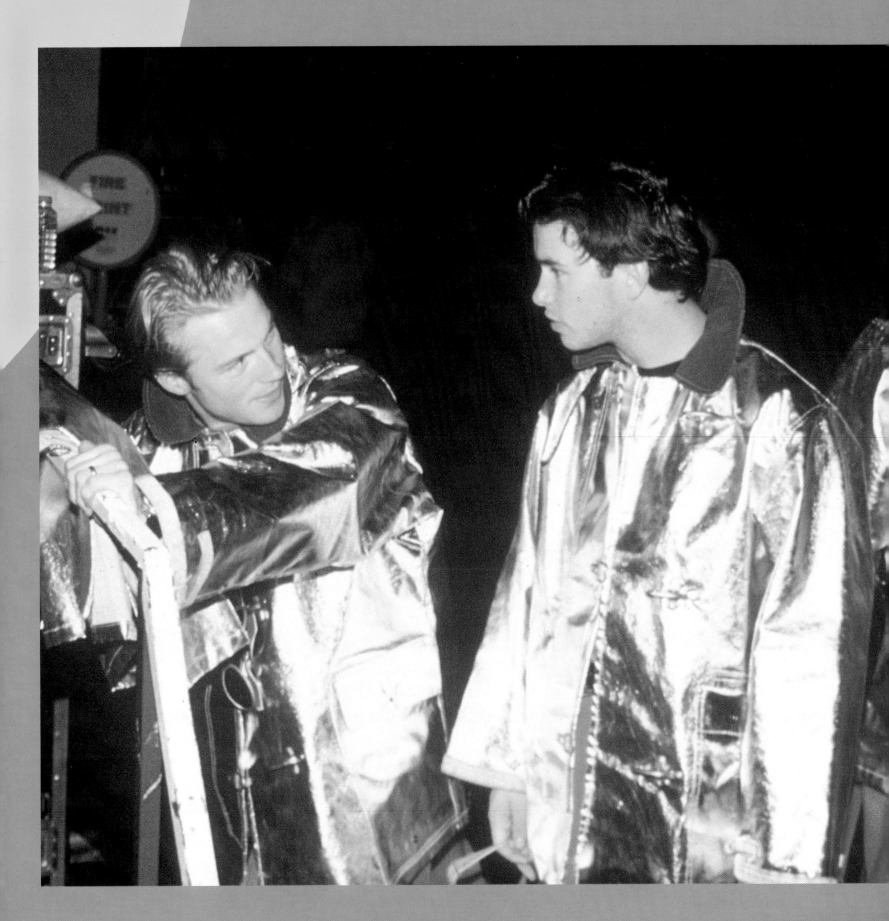

and has a minor role in Madonna's movie, Evita - admonishes Ronan for not turning up in the bar the previous night to buy her a drink.

"I was there, honestly, I bought your sisters a drink," he pleads.

On to the rehearsal room where minutes later there's a minor drama when burly Keith connects a kick to Ronan's head during a dance movement that goes wrong.

A pack of ice is instantly in demand thanks to the pitter patter of tiny feet. The stork has been working overtime and a new era is about to dawn for Keith and Mikey with the imminent arrival of their babies.

Keith's little bundle of joy, Jordan, was late entering this mortal world and played a big role in disrupting the intensive rehearsals. Interviews with various publications were also slotted in, taking time out of their day.

On the days they did rehearse, they

## "OBVIOUSLY BOYS WILL BE BOYS AND THEY CAN START ACTING A BIT GIDDY AND SILLY, BUT THEY KNOW WHEN IT'S TIME TO BE SERIOUS AGAIN BECAUSE OF THE FILTHY LOOK I GIVE THEM."

and Ronan sits down for half an hour holding it to an area around his left eye and praying that it doesn't balloon into a monster ball. It didn't, incidentally.

It's all part of the frenetic activities behind the scenes on the eve of their extensive '96 tour of the UK.

The schedule for the rehearsals has also gone out the window because there are other dramas going on...

kicked off around 11am and ran for two hours before breaking for lunch. The work started again at 2pm and they usually wrapped up around 4pm. But there's no such thing as a 'normal' day for the mega-group.

"I haven't had a normal day in three years," Ronan pants, as he towels the sweat from his body at the end of another arduous workout on the dance front.

Hot-shot choreographer Melinda McKenna, who has worked with the likes of East 17, Deuce and Louise, puts the Boyz through their paces. "They generally behave very well and take their instruction in a professional manner," Melinda says.

"Normally there's a lot of fun involved in what we do and that's the way it should be. You should be able to enjoy your work, even though it may involve a lot of effort and commitment."

Watching the guys build up their new steps and movements, it's amazing how much they've progressed since their early days.

Melinda is busy jotting down notes as she slots in some changes and improvements to enhance the look of the show. She says: "I'm constantly coming up with new things. Watching them physically rehearse a new routine gives me the chance to develop little things that give it a new dimension."

With the experience they've gained in the last couple of years, the Boyz now have their own input into the live show.

Melinda says: "I sit down with them now and work out the steps that they're comfortable with and it also gives them a chance to put their stamp on the dancing. Since they're the ones doing it, they need to be happy and comfortable with the set."

to be done because you've only got your hotel bedroom to go back to."

In the early days they snapped up every opportunity to spend time in their native city, but now the magnetic attraction isn't as strong.

In fact, they would have been rehearsing in London if Keith and Mikey hadn't been heading for Dadzone.

Steve: "Keith and Mikey didn't know when their babies were going to be born and they wanted to be at home

Although it's a high-tech, state-of-the-art studio, hit producer Ray Hedges has introduced a very homely feel with a nice rest area and kitchen and lots of natural light.

Ray, who co-writes and produces the group with his partner Martin Brannigan, worked with Take That in the early days and he's dead impressed with Boyzone.

Perched in a corner like a proud dad watching the Boyz work on a new track, Ray reveals: "There's something about Boyzone that's exciting. They're very distinctive, not your average boy band.

"I think the fact they're Irish also brings a lot of character to the group. You know what the Irish are like, just different."

It all started on a huge high the first week. The Boyz were buzzing with excitement over learning new routines and developing a different production to last year's live experience.

However, their energy levels were beginning to dramatically drop towards the end of the second week.

"That's quite normal for groups," Melinda explains. "But I'm thrilled with their progress. They can do things now that they were never able to do when I first met them."

Working at home in Dublin means that the Boyz get to hang out with their families for a while. But they also find that there are too many distractions which affect the way they operate.

Ronan: "When you're at home you're always thinking 'Can we get out at six or whatever because I've got to meet this person or that person?'

"When you're away you work better and concentrate on the job that has

Ray co-ordinates the songwriting and brings out the best in the Boyz.

"Their input is very refreshing. Lyrically they're very good and they also come up with melodies. They

when something happened, so that's how we ended up rehearsing in Dublin. I prefer to work in England."

Most of the album was recorded over a period of three months in a very pleasant studio outside London and overlooking a river.

Its exact location can't be disclosed to avoid an invasion of fans, but Boyzone loved it there because it's a sort of home from home.

have the best instrument possible for writing with, which is a good voice. "Ronan has got a very distinctive voice. It's very soulful and distorted. Steve has a very high and pure soulful voice, so you've got two conflicting textures which is useful."

One day as they are sitting at a keyboard writing with Ray and Martin, they find an African drum rhythm which turns on the Boyz. Using the distinctive groove, they start building up a song, introducing Irish pipes and other features and there's a great buzz in the studio as it comes together.

But creating songs isn't always easy for them. It's a lot like doing your school work sometimes.

Ronan: "Sometimes you just don't feel up to it and there's no point in doing it if you're not up to it."

Like many composers, Ronan and Steve find that their creative juices flow more easily late into the night.

Steve: "It's definitely much easier late at night. I'll work till 2am no problem and I get loads done. Most of the writing is done in the studio, but we do some on the road as well."

Next best thing to being on stage for Steve is working in the recording studio. He feels right at home there and obviously gets a real thrill when he's recording his self-penned songs.

Steve: "On the B-side of 'Coming Home' there's a song called 'Close To You'. I wrote the melody of that and I

wrote the chorus. I wrote it in Germany when we were doing a show for charity. It came together when we had a little time to spare.

"I was actually thinking along the lines of Walt Disney. If you listen, the chorus is really Walt Disney-ish. I wanted to sing a Walt Disney type of vibe to it.

confident now. In the early days they were intimidated by the technology and the whole recording process.

They also weren't aware of their own strengths at the beginning and allowed others to dictate to them. Not anymore.

Steve: "When we started out and before we linked up with Ray, I was

more confident."

Ronan: "The studio people can tell him he can sing something or he can't, but he knows himself what he can do. We've been around three years now and we've gained a lot of experience, so we can put our foot down if we disagree with the way things are done. We don't have to apologise anymore."

As the album comes together, the Boyz are clearly delighted with the way it's turning out.

At the end of one long day, Ronan sits back and listens to a playback.

He closes his eyes and allows the recordings to fill up his senses. At the end he lets out a huge sigh and smiles.

"You can feel we're more mature," he says. "It's a very different sound, a different album to Said And Done, but it still has that Boyzone trademark once you hear the voices. Whether it's Steven or whoever singing, it's Boyzone.

"We haven't gone for a radical change of style. But there are some really beautiful songs there. I'm really proud of what we've done."

# "In the last year, we've seen so many things and we've learnt so many things. We've met people who've influenced us and you can see that in some of the songs."

And I was really, really pleased because I didn't know it was going to go on the B-side."

In the studio the Boyz are a lot more

asked to sing in a way that was not me singing. It was not the way I sing. Now I know what my voice can do and what range I can reach and I'm much

**"FIVE LADS FROM THE**

**NORTHSIDE OF DUBLIN,**

**HAVING A LAUGH,**

Pop music's hottest young performer - he's only nineteen - is in the middle of another year of mayhem. There are times when the pressure of life in a supergroup shows in his features.

Ronan is the youngest member of the group, but the rest of the Boyz often refer to Ro as their 'Big Daddy'. And for a good reason. He possesses a sense of maturity beyond his years. He's **Mr Competent. Mr Dependable. Mr Conscientious.**

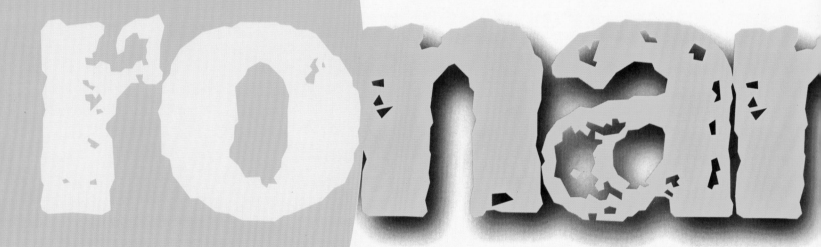

**HAVING A GOOD TIME,**

**ENJOYING OURSELVES.**

**TRAVELLING THE WORLD WITH**

**MATES. THAT'S WHAT IT IS."**

The other Boyz all agree that having 'Ro' around makes them feel secure. They know they're in safe hands.

Ronan reflects on his character traits: "I'm an awful worrier. It's something I've inherited from my mother. Like mother, like son. She has me the way I am. I feel the pressure because I take a lot of things upon myself. Doing stuff that I shouldn't have to do. I can't leave things to other people. I have to do them myself."

The 'boy' I first met when Boyzone were being groomed for stardom three years ago bears no resemblance to the muscle-bound hunk now sitting before me on the plane.

Back then, Ronan was a slightly built young teenager, dreaming of superstardom with the newly created group, Boyzone, as he sipped from a mug

RONAN KEATING

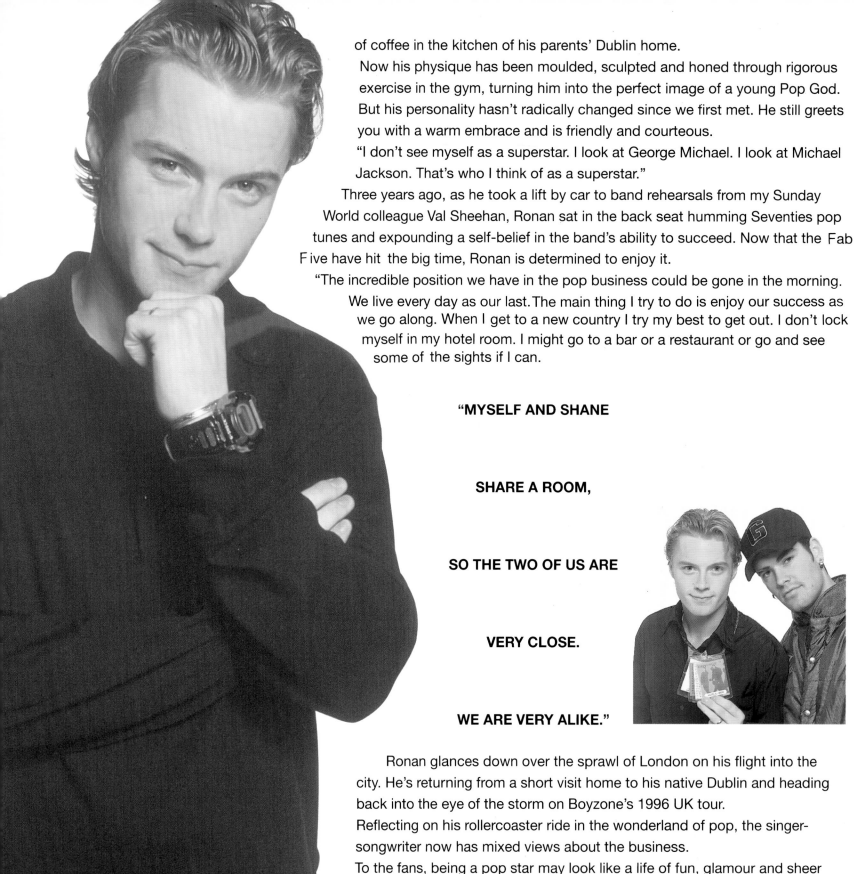

of coffee in the kitchen of his parents' Dublin home.

Now his physique has been moulded, sculpted and honed through rigorous exercise in the gym, turning him into the perfect image of a young Pop God. But his personality hasn't radically changed since we first met. He still greets you with a warm embrace and is friendly and courteous.

"I don't see myself as a superstar. I look at George Michael. I look at Michael Jackson. That's who I think of as a superstar."

Three years ago, as he took a lift by car to band rehearsals from my Sunday World colleague Val Sheehan, Ronan sat in the back seat humming Seventies pop tunes and expounding a self-belief in the band's ability to succeed. Now that the Fab Five have hit the big time, Ronan is determined to enjoy it.

"The incredible position we have in the pop business could be gone in the morning. We live every day as our last. The main thing I try to do is enjoy our success as we go along. When I get to a new country I try my best to get out. I don't lock myself in my hotel room. I might go to a bar or a restaurant or go and see some of the sights if I can.

**"MYSELF AND SHANE**

**SHARE A ROOM,**

**SO THE TWO OF US ARE**

**VERY CLOSE.**

**WE ARE VERY ALIKE."**

Ronan glances down over the sprawl of London on his flight into the city. He's returning from a short visit home to his native Dublin and heading back into the eye of the storm on Boyzone's 1996 UK tour.

Reflecting on his rollercoaster ride in the wonderland of pop, the singer-songwriter now has mixed views about the business.

To the fans, being a pop star may look like a life of fun, glamour and sheer pleasure. And while all those essential ingredients do exist, there is a huge price to be extracted.

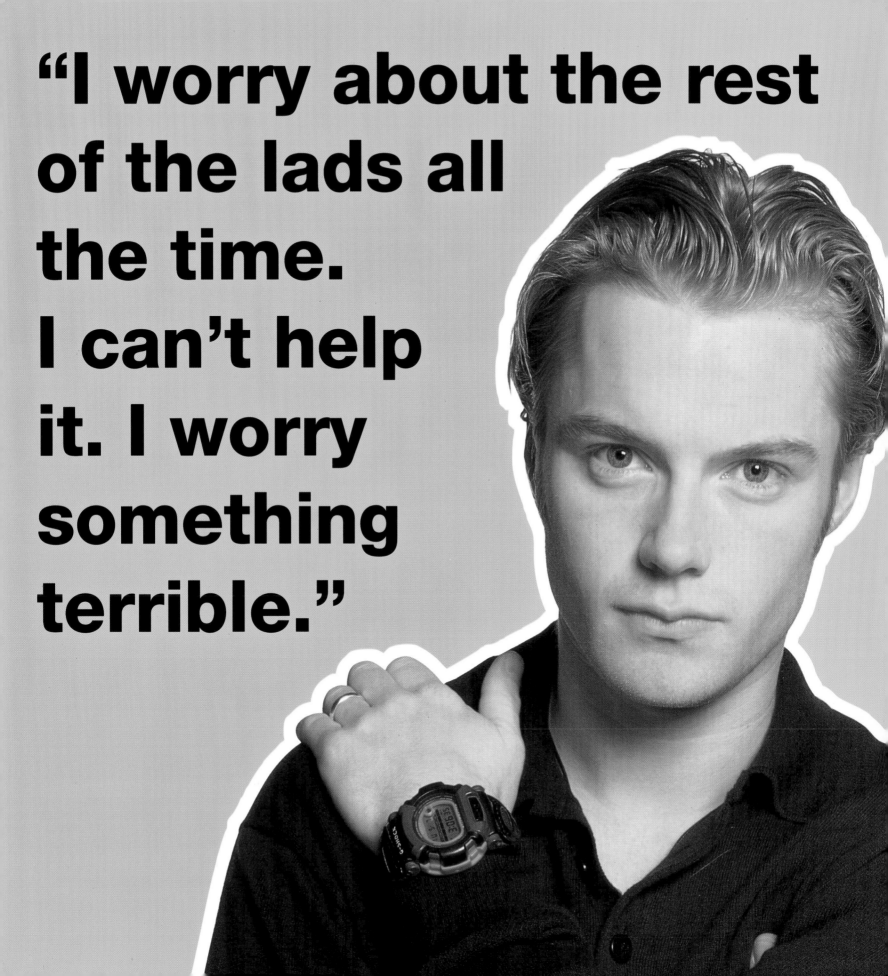

"I worry about the rest of the lads all the time. I can't help it. I worry something terrible."

Ronan is acutely aware of the cost he's paid for his privileged position in life. The loss of privacy. The gruelling, non-stop work regime. The unceasing demands on him by people from all walks of life.

It finally hit him like an express train at the start of the year when he returned from a well-earned holiday in America. After tasting freedom and anonymity in a country where Boyzone are still an unknown quantity, Ronan found himself battling with the demons in his head.

For the first time in his short but eventful life, Ronan was gripped with a sense of panic and fear as he faced up to his career in the fast lane again.

His burning ambition to live the life of a pop star had been quenched and he found himself struggling to re-start the fire.

"I never want to experience that again. We'd had a crazy work year in '95. We worked non-stop from the start of the year until December. It was brilliant. I'm not complaining. I loved it.

"But in December, after we'd finished two shows at Dublin's Point Depot, none of us could take any more.

We needed a break. I went to New York for two weeks and had a ball. I lost myself totally.

"It was like a breath of fresh air going to a country where I could become anonymous again, because nobody knows us there. I was just plain 'Ro' and it was brilliant. I went skiing with my brothers and sister. We had such a great time that I forgot I was in any band.

"The trouble started when I came home. I couldn't settle back into my life. Usually I can adapt very easily

to things like that.

"But after the freedom I had enjoyed on my holidays, it was difficult to go back into the goldfish bowl and become public property again.

"I came home from the States in late January and for the first few weeks in February I didn't know what was going on. I was so confused.

"But eventually I came around and I'm now back to myself, thank God.

# It was weird. I don't want that to happen again. It was kind of a scary feeling,

to be honest."

Growing up in a pop group has given Ronan a broad perspective on life. Unlike most young men of his age, he has been afforded the opportunity to travel and experience other countries and cultures. Living a jet-set lifestyle can take its toll on personal relationships, so the young star is determined to just have some fun along the way and wait until the hectic pace of his life slows down before committing himself to a lifetime partner.

"Relationships are very difficult. Like, I was going out with a girl at the beginning and it was very hard because I was travelling away so much. It wasn't fair on her and it wasn't fair on me because on the road you get lonely and you need somebody.

"She wasn't there and I couldn't be there for her. It just hurt too much. So we called it a day. It was a mutual thing. That was in the early stages of my career.

"It was for the best because I can work better now. I work better on my own. I try not to get tied in emotionally to someone while this is going on, but it's very hard. There are times when you meet the person and they're just right and there's nothing you can do about the way your heart feels. I'm a very sensitive person. I can see through people very easily and I can tell what they are like.

"But I look at it from the perspective of being a young guy with his whole life ahead of him, so there's no need to rush things. I didn't use to be like that, but I am now."

## "I USED TO BE VERY NAIVE. I KNOW I'M ONLY 19, BUT I'VE LEARNED SO MUCH. THE PEOPLE AROUND ME ARE ALL OLDER, SO THEY'VE TAUGHT ME A LOT."

Like every celebrity, Ronan has to tread carefully with the females who express an interest in him. He's constantly faced with the age-old dilemma of personalities - 'Does she love me for myself or because of who I am?'

"I can see through the girls who are only into me because I'm in Boyzone. That's very easy to tell. We're extremely wary of things like that. It's a very scary thing.

"I may eventually end up with someone in the business. That could very well happen because there's a mutual understanding. They know how you feel, being in the business, and you know how they feel and the difficulties that go with their lives. So it's easier to adapt to each other.

"But meeting the right person is not something you can plan coldly. When it happens, it happens and it could be anyone from any walk of life."

MILLIONAIRE. A status we all aspire to, but few of us will ever realise. It's a term that may soon apply to the Boyz as their career grows and grows and new territories open up to them.

Ronan has ear-marked a slice of his fortune for his dream home:

fortune for his dream home:

"I'D LIKE A BIG, STATELY MANSION. A REALLY OLD HOUSE WITH A LONG, TREE-LINED DRIVE UP TO IT. WE ALL LOVE CARS: I'D LIKE TO HAVE A COUPLE OF OLD ONES OUT ON THE FORECOURT. I LOVE OLD CLASSICS."

One of the best things about earning serious money is that you can afford to indulge yourself in your personal pleasures and one of Ronan's vices is... clothes. Designer clothes, to be precise.

"I'm a bit of a sucker for the clothes. I spend a lot of my money on them. Designer label victim? That's me. Totally. I like a lot of different designers. Dolce & Gabbana are one of my favourites. I like good quality clothes that I feel good in. That's important for me.

"I wear something for a while and then I want something new. You open my wardrobe and there's so many clothes that I've never worn. The tags are still on them, which is very sad! But I do that. I buy something and I forget I have it. Clothes are one of the luxuries I allow myself."

Having been the recipient of mind-

**"I've grown up a lot in the last three years. I had to. The five of us had to. It's a crazy game. It's a crazy business."**

blowing adulation from fans all around Europe, Southeast Asia and Australia, topping the charts, picking up an armful of awards and appearing on major TV shows, how difficult is it for Ronan to get a thrill nowadays?

"I enjoy the simple things in life and that's what's important to me. I like going to the movies. Eating good food. Having a laugh. We have a 'mental hour' now and again in the band where we just laugh and laugh."

K E A T I N G

"I LOVE TO LAUGH.

JUST TO BE HAPPY. AND

I LOVE PEOPLE AROUND ME

TO BE HAPPY. IT BOTHERS

ME WHEN THEY'RE NOT."

IT'S THE EARLY HOURS OF THE MORNING IN A HOTEL CORRIDOR AND A SINISTER-LOOKING FIGURE IS ACTING SUSPICIOUSLY.
THE CHARACTER WITH THE LARGE FRAME IS PROWLING FROM BEDROOM DOOR TO BEDROOM DOOR, REMOVING NOTICES FROM THE DOOR KNOBS AND REPLACING THEM WITH NEW ONES.

**"WE DO HAVE LAUGHS WITH EACH OTHER. WE CAN BE QUITE CHILDISH AT TIMES. WE ALL KNOW EACH OTHER'S GOOD SIDES. WE ALL KNOW HOW TO CHEER EACH OTHER UP. BUT WE ALSO KNOW HOW TO WIND EACH OTHER UP."**

ON THE ROAD

It transpires that the bedrooms are occupied by three of the other four members of Boyzone, Ronan, Shane and Mikey. Before hotel security is alerted to the strange goings-on, Keith is revealed as the mystery stalker.

There's a smirk on his face and a twinkle in his eye that spells mischief... and that's what he's up to. Keith is springing a breakfast surprise on Ronan, Shane and Mikey. Steve generally doesn't eat breakfast.

The three Boyz had retired to bed about 20 minutes earlier, tired and hungry and looking forward to a nice big fry-up when it's time to start another hectic day. They've left out their order for 'the works'... a tasty grill of sausages, bacon, black and white pudding, eggs, mushrooms and beans. Mouthwatering stuff, indeed.

But Keith is up to his old tricks. He's altering each individual's order before the hotel staff come to collect them.

So, instead of a delicious fry, the other three Boyz are going to be sitting down to a breakfast of muesli, natural yogurt and kippers!

Thrilled with his night's work, Keith retires to his own bedroom and looks forward to all hell breaking loose the following morning.

"Keith's not only a joker, he's a trouble-maker," Shane says the following day when it's revealed who caused the breakfast disaster. "Whenever there's an argument, you can be sure that he's at the centre of it. But he's harmless.

"He does make us laugh, but he's a nightmare when he's tired. When he's tired he gets loud and he messes and just goes for it. If you're in a bad mood, he'll play on that. He can really push it."

When I mention this criticism to him later, Keith instantly puts his hands up and pleads guilty, your honour. "When I'm

# "We all used to share rooms at one time, but we decided that wasn't a good idea because everyone needs their own bit of private space..."

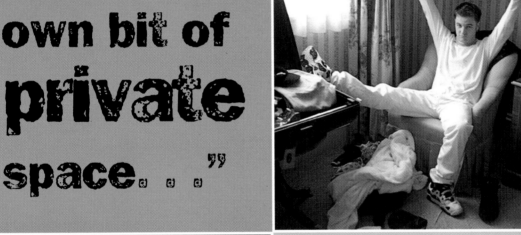

feelings easier than some of them. Sometimes if I feel it's not being reciprocated, instead of trying to tell them how I feel about them, I end up doing things that have the opposite effect.

"Myself and Mikey have a row every now and then. We rub off each other a little bit. But at the end of the day, if I walked outside the building and someone was giving Mikey grief, I'd run to his defence."

All the Boyz have different personalities, but in general they appear to gel well together.

Mikey says: "Sometimes it can be a bit difficult. Not that there's a personality clash, but when you put people together 24 hours a day, seven days a week, working, eating and doing everything together, it's bound to have a negative effect somewhere along the line.

At 3pm one Saturday in a

bored everybody knows about it. Like I'd be, er, getting on people's nerves and just being... Keith, basically."

Keith is the catalyst for a lot of mayhem as the group work their way through the tour. But he does help to defuse a lot of pent-up pressure and stress with his wayward antics.

He says: "There are times when I need to know that the boys love me as much as I love them. I show my

Cambridge hotel during the tour, Steve is found in the dining room, tucking into spicy chicken wings and barbeque spare ribs.

Keith is working out in the hotel's gymnasium, Mikey is sleeping and both Ronan and Shane are returning from commitments in London.

Two of the waitresses come over to Steve, seeking his autograph. With sticky fingers, he gracefully obliges their requests. Then they try to blag some tickets for the show that night. Steve says he'll see what he can do. This is Steve's first meal of the day.

"I only have two meals a day," he says. "I try not to put on weight and sometimes I have to diet. With the lifestyle we lead, you tend to eat a lot of rich foods.

"Sometimes the lads would go for a Big Mac and I'd say 'No, I'll have a salad sandwich or something.' I never used to take vitamins, but now I take

Royal Jelly which has done me the world of good.

"This year we wanted to do extra special things with ourselves. We want to look really good. So we all went out and bought clothes and we're taking care of ourselves.

"The dancing keeps us fit because it's so tough. Our new dancing is just incredible. It's so funky."

John Duffy, Keith's 17-year-old brother, is on the tour and he joins Steve at the table. "Do you think Keith would kill me if I ordered a steak and put it on his room number?" he asks. Steve laughs and orders steak for John, who has been flown over from Dublin to join the Boyzone road show as a special treat for his birthday.

Keith's life on the road is built around the gym. He loves his workouts. When the other guys are having a lie-in, Keith will be found in what many would consider the 'torture chamber', working his way through his daily routine of exercise.

He says: "Whenever we have any spare time, I'll spend it down in the gym doing a couple of hours. If I don't keep training all the time I put on weight because I have a slow metabolism.

"I always feel better about myself after a session in the gym. If you're feeling tired it's a great way of burning up the negative energy and gaining a lot of positive energy which helps you get through the day.

"I do this thing called the treadmill challenge. It's a running machine and you can do a challenge, fight the machine on different levels to build up stamina. At the end of that, you feel great and refreshed and you have no worries in the world, y'know."

Old Rip Van Winkle himself, Mikey, grabs his forty winks at every available opportunity. Even if he wasn't in a demanding job, Mikey reckons he would still need more sleep than the average person.

He says: "I don't know whether it's a lack of something, but I just sleep all the time. It's not only me, my brother is a terrible person for sleeping as well. We fall asleep anywhere."

Mikey doesn't have any personal fitness regime or particular diet.

"Touring can be pretty gruelling, y'know, and with all the dancing we do I think it's enough to keep me fit.

"Performing night after night, you'd want to be eating everything you can get into you. Chocolate as well as good food. You need things like that in your system to keep your energy levels up."

There's a boredom factor to contend with as they hang around in venues during sound checks or video shoots. Shane says: "We

cope with it in different ways. It depends on where you are, really. If I'm bored I go and find doors that lead somewhere, check out the building... just silly little things like that to keep you amused."

Their tour bus coasts along the motorway, a semi-home from home on wheels. It's got just about everything you need to fill in the time travelling.

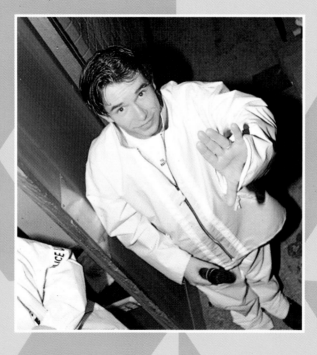

There's a little sitting-room at the back, complete with TV and video. Steve can be found there watching Sister Act 2 for the 100th time. He loves Whoopi Goldberg. When the others arrive and discover what's on the TV screen yet again, there's a communal roar of disapproval. Searching through the videos, which

were supplied with the bus, they decide to check out Roy Chubby Brown, a British comedian who wouldn't be allowed near a live TV show because he paints the air blue.

Shane reckons some of Chubby's jokes are 'very Irish', but in general the Boyz are only mildly amused by the outrageous comic. Usually, it takes them some time to come down from their adrenalin high after a show, so they watch a video before drifting off to their bunks at different stages.

Occasionally there are glitzy showbiz bashes to attend and it was on one of those occasions that Ronan finally got the opportunity to meet his own idol, George Michael.

It was at the Capital 98 FM awards ceremony in the UK, which George Michael attends every year. Ronan, however, had no idea that his hero was going to be there... and his jaw dropped when he spotted him at the next table.

Like every fan, Ronan was determined to seize the opportunity and introduce himself. And he was thrilled when he discovered that George Michael knew all about him. Ronan revealed: "George said

'I love your record 'Father And Son'. Myself and my mother were talking about it. My mum said "Look at that guy, he's only a young fella and he's singing to his son. How can that be?" And I said to her, "Nah, mum, don't be silly. It's him singing to his father."'

"It was just so weird to think that George Michael was having a conversation about myself and Boyzone at home with his mum. Ah, he was brilliant. I was just in awe of him. I was shaking big time, big time. Now I understand how the fans feel about us. It's weird, but that's the way it is."

During daylight hours on the road, it's rare to find the lads without a mobile phone attached to their ears. They're either doing phone interviews en route to gigs, or else catching up on the news from home. Telephone calls are their biggest expense on the road.

The only band member without a mobile phone this year is Keith. He didn't pay his bill!

Keith revealed: "I was in Denmark on a promotional trip and I decided to phone home. I called my family and a few mates and I didn't think I was that long on the line. But when I got the bill it was over £500! I didn't pay it, so I was cut off."

There's a knock on Keith's

bedroom door. "Why aren't you down in the lobby, mate? The bus is ready to leave." It's the voice of Barrie Knight, their personal security man.

Keith: "I'll be down in a few minutes. I'm just finishing up something here."

Barrie (adopting a more authoritative tone): "Downstairs now, Keith. OK?"

Security is a necessary part of the Boyzone camp. Barrie Knight is not the sort of mean animal you normally associate with the job. He's a mild-mannered Frank Bruno-type with a good line in humour, but he's not to be crossed. Barrie looked after Matt and Luke Goss during their Bros-mania days, so he's no stranger to the mayhem surrounding boy groups.

The Boyz respect his authority and usually do what he tells them because they know it's for their own safety and protection.

Barrie says: "I'm no bully, but they know I've got to do a job. My main job is to get them in and out of buses and buildings without incident. Sometimes I'll also go and perk them up if they're feeling down. It's a bit like being a nanny as well."

"WE ALWAYS SEEM TO SPEND

ALL OUR TIME TRYING TO

CATCH UP ON SLEEP."

SHANE LYNCH

THE TRADEMARK
SHAVED RIGHT EYEBROW
SAYS IT ALL. SHANE LYNCH
STRIVES FOR INDIVIDUALITY.

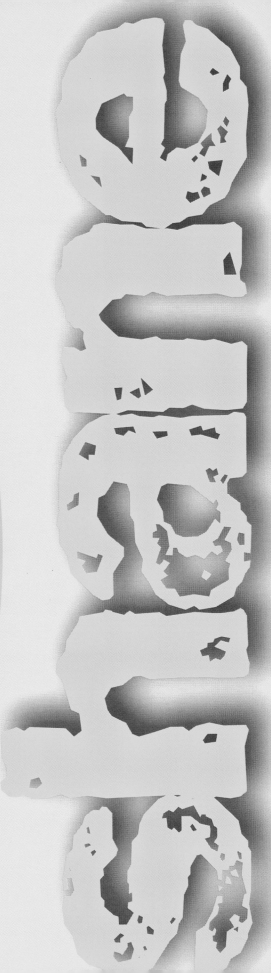

Back a few years ago when he was working his way through the turmoil of adolescence and battling to find his own identity, Shane had a flamboyant streak in him.

Before he started splitting his eyebrow, the star in the making had already been dying his brown hair black... his favourite colour.

Later he even forked out his hard-earned cash - a whopping £150 - to have his short hair transformed into a mass of tiny braided 'sticks'.

His style of dress also displayed his drive to be unique. Growing up in a relatively small city like Dublin, Shane was afraid to be too adventurous in the clothes he selected.

One of the advantages of becoming a star is that you're expected to be different and there's a higher level of tolerance of both the actions and style of showbiz people. Shane is now revelling in his new-found freedom to express himself.

He still has has that shy, vulnerable appearance, almost in the way that Princess Di might look at you. But behind the sheepish exterior there now lurks a very confident, self-assured young man.

Sprawled across a

**"I CAN SOAK UP**

**A LOT OF**

**PRESSURE.**

**I JUST TAKE IT**

**IN MY STRIDE.**

**I'M VERY, VERY**

**EASY-GOING."**

"I shine quite a lot because I wear

a lot of different colours, more so

than the other guys in the group."

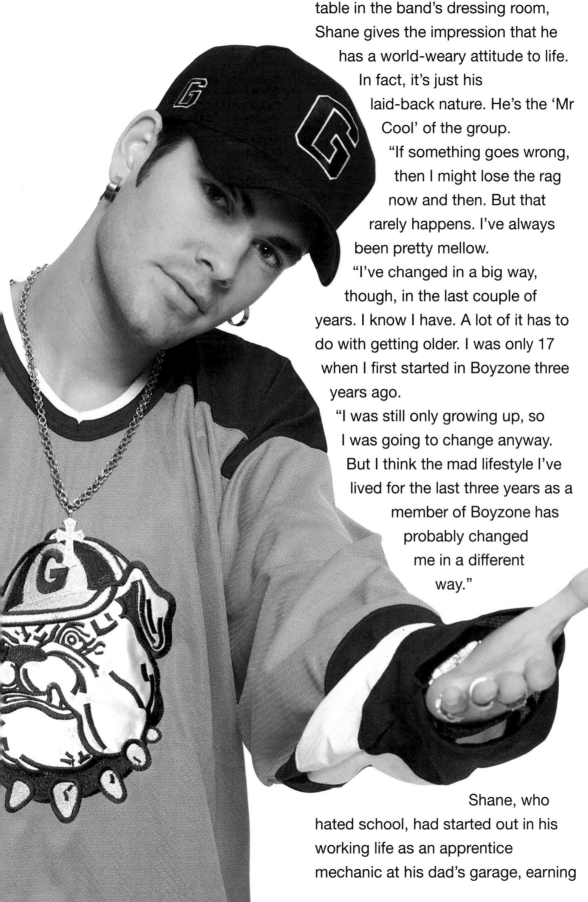

table in the band's dressing room, Shane gives the impression that he has a world-weary attitude to life. In fact, it's just his laid-back nature. He's the 'Mr Cool' of the group.

"If something goes wrong, then I might lose the rag now and then. But that rarely happens. I've always been pretty mellow.

"I've changed in a big way, though, in the last couple of years. I know I have. A lot of it has to do with getting older. I was only 17 when I first started in Boyzone three years ago.

"I was still only growing up, so I was going to change anyway. But I think the mad lifestyle I've lived for the last three years as a member of Boyzone has probably changed me in a different way."

Shane, who hated school, had started out in his working life as an apprentice mechanic at his dad's garage, earning £50 a week. His current role in life is light years away from the normal routine of a nine to five job.

"When I first joined the group I was a very, very shy bloke. Walking around Dublin I could not be the way I always wanted to be. I wanted to dress in a certain way, but I didn't have the courage to do it. I felt I had to conform and be like everyone else. Now I'm a lot different. I'm more out-going."

That fresh confidence emerged when he strutted his funky stuff on the catwalk during a charity fashion show in his native city. The star-studded event featured supermodels like Naomi Campbell and Eva Herzigova. But it was Shane who stole the show and made the headlines when he dropped his pants to reveal his skimpy briefs. He later explained that he'd spent the afternoon drinking with wild men of pop Robbie Williams and Liam Gallagher and that had inspired his show of exhibitionism.

One fan later wrote to UK pop magazine Smash Hits asking 'How come your lunch box is bigger than Linford Christie's?' Well, there's really no answer to that one!

As a teenager, it wasn't just his sense of fashion that made Shane realise how he differed from the other kids in his neighbourhood. While they were tuning in to the contemporary pop and rock hits, Shane was getting turned on by rhythm and blues, reggae and hip hop.

**Standing six foot tall and possessing stunning good looks, it's easy to see why Shane is a 'dream boat' to millions of teenage girls.**

But touring and performing around the world can take its toll on a performer's health and looks. The dizzy round of planes, buses, hotels and concert venues can involve lots of snacks and drinks that pile on the pounds. Shane reckons he's lucky to have a metabolism that burns off excess fat and keeps him a lean machine.

He's not a wild party animal behind the scenes. You'll usually find him hitting the sack before Steve, who has the reputation of being the quietest member of the group.

What about home life? Having spent so much time away from home

# "I'M VERY LUCKY THAT I DON'T PUT ON WEIGHT. BUT WHEN I'M ON STAGE I WORK HARD. I RECKON IT'S THE DANCING THAT KEEPS ME FIT AS WELL."

base himself outside his homeland. "I'll always have my bedroom at my Ma's house, I know that. But as far as living in Ireland is concerned, I don't know. I wouldn't necessarily buy a house there straight away. I know if this group does finish, I won't live in Ireland for two or more years. I'll wait until all the mania passes over and things cool down. Then I may move back. Ireland isn't the sort of place where you can slip out of the public eye and do things in private. It's just too small.

"I'd live in the States. It's just a mad place. I loved Miami when we were over there doing promotion, but I'll probably live in New York or Los Angeles for a while. I like the idea of being able to get lost over there. It's big and wild and I'm into that."

He's the guy millions of girls fancy and loads of blokes envy, but where affairs of the heart are concerned,

during the past two years, the attraction of Dublin isn't as strong as it used to be. Shane has been around the world and he now realises that he could set up a new life almost anywhere. The money he'll eventually earn from the phenomenal success of Boyzone will give Shane the option of choosing any lifestyle he desires. He knows that there'll always been a warm welcome for him in the family home, but he may

Shane has his own problems. While he admits that it is possible to have a relationship and juggle a high-flying pop career at the same time, the star has to question the motives of most of the stunning young girls who express an interest in him.

"I'm wary of girls coming on to me nowadays. I have to stop and think, does she want me because I'm famous or is she into me as a person?"

So how should a girl behave if she hopes to be in with a fighting chance to nab the eligible bachelor? Basically, ignore him and he'll come running.

"If I see a girl I'm interested in and she's not too bothered, I'll chase her like mad to see if I can get her. If she's not interested I'll go for her. It's the chase I'm after."

While Shane has a loyal core of girl fans in his native Dublin, he finds that some of the girls he encounters in nightclubs when he hits the club scene at home during his time off are

snooty towards him.

"The girls at home in the nightclubs can be worse than the fellas for slagging you off. You just can't win with them. If you sit in a corner they'll say, 'Oh, look at him, who does he think he is? He's too cool to get up and dance.'

"If you do get up and dance it's 'Look at him, letting everyone know he's here. Who does he think he is?' It's

usually the girls more than the fellas that I get that kind of reaction from."

He shrugs: "But I just ignore it all. I don't make a point of staying away from the places where I used to hang out before joining Boyzone. The only place I don't go to is the cinema complex for security reasons, because of the crowds. But, in general, I go wherever I went before."

"ANY GIRL WHO COMES ON TO ME

I'LL CHARM AND HAVE A LAUGH WITH.

BUT AT THE END OF THE NIGHT I'M

GOING HOME ON MY OWN."

BOYZONE SURVEYED THE DISMAL CLUB SCENE FROM THE STAGE AND THEIR MORALE PLUNGED TO ROCK BOTTOM. THE VENUE WAS VIRTUALLY EMPTY, BUT THE SHOW HAD TO GO ON.

**"THERE'S NO**

**NERVES AROUND AN**

**HOUR BEFORE THE**

**CONCERT.**

**IT HAPPENS**

**WHEN YOU'RE**

**BEHIND THE CURTAIN**

**WAITING TO GO OUT"**

They summoned up every ounce of courage and tried desperately to pluck some enthusiasm from the depths of their despair as they fought what was clearly going to be a losing battle at the hands of a hostile crowd.

The venue was set in a rural town of Ireland and the audience was of a more mature vintage than your typical boy band followers.

It was the early days of Boyzone on the road and it was a baptism of fire as they came face to face with the realities of life in the showbiz world.

As the missiles were hurled up on stage, the Boyz must surely have wondered if their career was over before it even began.

Looking back now, Boyzone see the merits of their tortuous route to the top of the pop ladder. It has helped to steel them against the turbulence that they may encounter from time to time... and it has given them a genuine appreciation of their success and good fortune.

Mikey says: "It was quite obvious in some of the venues we played around Ireland at the start

of our career that the crowd wasn't a Boyzone following. It was tough. It was so tough. We played in some of the worst little holes around Ireland. We played to big crowds and we played to ridiculously small crowds.

"A lot of the venues were nightclubs and, obviously, there were a lot of drunk people there. They'd be throwing things up on stage and hurling abuse. Now, I'm not the sort of fella who can take that, but I just had to bite my lip and go on with the show."

Boyzone would never have been born if it wasn't for one man's dream of launching an Irish boy band to pop superstardom. But the Boyz are adamant that once destiny

intervened in the guise of pop guru Louis Walsh, their sheer hard work took care of the rest.

Keith: "There are a lot of bands that haven't made it and that's because they didn't have the dedication and commitment that we have. Success wasn't handed to us on a plate. We gave over our whole lives and worked ourselves to the bone to make it happen.

"Our management and the record

Looking back on their early efforts, the Boyz cringe with embarrassment. Like the time they appeared on Ireland's top TV chat show, the Late Late Show, which is hosted by Gay Byrne.

They were introduced on the chat show as the next Irish pop sensations, but they didn't even have a proper dance routine and ended up looking rather silly when they were asked to perform.

Steve: "Oh yeah, when I look back at some of the early things we did, I cringe. I go, 'Oh no, that's not me!' I laugh a lot. When I see us on the Late Late Show that first time I just

"WE NEVER REGARDED OURSELVES AS POP STARS AND WE'VE NEVER HAD AN ATTITUDE PROBLEM. WE WERE UNSURE OF OURSELVES STARTING OUT, BUT WE WEREN'T AFRAID TO LOOK FOR ADVICE AND GUIDANCE AND WE LISTENED TO WHAT PEOPLE TOLD US.."

company got the ball rolling. But, after that, we didn't take anything for granted. We did everything we were asked to do to make Boyzone the success it is today."

howl with laughter. I find it so, so funny. That TV appearance will always come back to haunt us. But you gotta make a start somewhere."

The 13th - an unlucky number for

some, but it's a memorable date in Boyzone's career.

Saturday, 13th July 1996... the day that Boyzone played the first of FOUR shows at Wembley Arena, their very first time performing at the top British venue.

The Boyz performed to a staggering 250,000 fans on their '96 U.K. tour, but Wembley was special.

It's every aspiring group's dream to star at Wembley and Boyzone made it a night of celebration, flying in their families from Ireland for the event. Ronan's sister Linda and brother Ger also made a transatlantic trek from New York to witness their kid brother's big moment.

As their massive tour bus roared up to Wembley on that balmy Saturday afternoon, the Boyz' hearts skipped a beat when they caught sight of their name proudly emblazoned in large letters above the front of the arena. Their moment of glory had finally arrived. Ronan's grin was as wide as the Pacific Ocean. "You imagine playing here, but I can't believe that we actually are," he gushed.

Keith tried to keep their excitement under control by playing down the significance of the moment.

"It's just another venue. It's just another show. You just gotta look at it like that," he said to his pals.

Their only previous experience of a Wembley show was when they went

**"I SAT ON STAGE SINGING FATHER AND SON AND FOR THE FIRST TIME I TOOK THE MONITOR OUT OF MY EAR AND HEARD THE WHOLE CROWD SINGING IT RIGHT BACK TO ME. IT BROUGHT MORE THAN A TEAR TO MY EYE, I CAN TELL YOU. IT WAS AN AMAZING EXPERIENCE."**

to see their pals MN8 support Janet Jackson there.

Former Bros star Matt Goss had put it into perspective for Ronan. Matt told him: "Wembley is sacred, y'know. The first time I walked into Wembley Arena it was just a different feeling to any other gig. Savour every moment of it."

It wasn't just teenage girls making the pilgrimage to Wembley that day. Bald men with pot-bellies and mums

Wembley was bigger than the early leg of the tour. It also had Sean Maguire, Peter Andre, Reel To Real, Kavana and Rebeka Ryan.

Backstage, the Boyz popped in and out of their plush dressing-room, which had expensive leather seating, a bathroom equipped with a jacuzzi and a TV and music system.

Keith arrived in with his mum and dad, Pat and Sean, to proudly show it off. "Look, leather seats and there's even

Steve discovered that he'd left a pair of stage trousers back in his hotel wardrobe. There was a frantic dash around to find a replacement.

An hour before they were due on stage, the Boyz were busy meeting lucky fans who had won competitions to see their idols in the flesh.

Among the giddy gathering were famous sextuplets, the Waltons... Hannah, Lucy, Ruth, Sarah, Kate and Jenny.

**"THIS IS A PROUD**

**MOMENT FOR US, BUT IF**

**IT WASN'T FOR YOU WE**

**WOULDN'T BE HERE."**

and dads were also making the journey to see their heroes The Eagles perform next door in Wembley Stadium.

Outside the Boyzone gig, eager fans were desperately trying to catch a glimpse of the Boyz. One young girl spotted Steve strolling around in his baseball cap and she promptly ran away shrieking with joy.

The Boyzone show that rolled into

a jacuzzi back there," he beamed.

Ronan was listening to Gary Barlow's new single, 'Forever Love', for the first time. "Oh man, that is beautiful," he enthused.

Steve was having his hair trimmed by their stylist, Alex Delves.

Outside, Shane, bedecked with gold rings and chains and sporting new hair extensions, was clowning around with Ronan's little nephew, Conal.

Out in the venue, the young fans were going into over-drive as the opening acts built up the atmosphere to fever pitch.

The shrill sound of whistles coupled with ear-piercing screams filled up the jam-packed arena as the minutes counted down to Boyzone's appearance.

Besotted fans were frantically waving banners declaring: 'Steve You're The Key To Our Lives' and 'We Love U4 Eternity, Boyzone'. And there was a cheeky one for Shane, which read: 'Shane, Show Us Your Lynchbox'.

Then the magic moment arrived and the five hunks marched up behind the stage looking dazzling in their silver fireman's jackets and red zipped trousers.

Their manager Louis Walsh followed them on to the stage to wish them good luck.

"It's a long way from Toghers in Naas," Keith shouted at him... a reference to their very first gig in a small Irish venue where there were only twenty people in the audience. Then, amid smoke and a thundering beat the Boyz blasted into action with 'Together,' merging from a cage to whip the fans into a frenzy... and send tears of joy streaming down the faces of their proud parents.

The arena erupted as the video screen showed the Boyz undressing and changing into different outfits

**RONAN: "WE WANT TO BE THE BIGGEST BAND WE CAN BE IN THE WORLD. BUT WE'VE GOT A LOT OF WORK TO DO BEFORE WE GET THERE."**

backstage during the performance. Back on stage there was a hiccup when Steve's microphone didn't work during a solo chorus. Keith put a comforting arm around him and mouthed: "Don't worry about it, pal." But it didn't matter because the crowd were oblivious to the minor drama. They were too busy screaming their heads off at Steve when he turned around and flashed them a smile that lit up the venue.

The Boys dedicated 'Coming Home Now' to "our mammies, daddies, brothers and sisters here tonight". And then, all too soon they headed into the final numbers, returning to perform 'A Different Beat' as their last encore.

As the mesmerised fans started filing out of the venue, the sweat-soaked Boyz, draped with towels and wearing dressing gowns, were already on the bus and heading into the night. Wembley had been conquered. Ronan said afterwards: "To play Wembley may not be the biggest gig in the world, but you know you're doing alright when you get it."

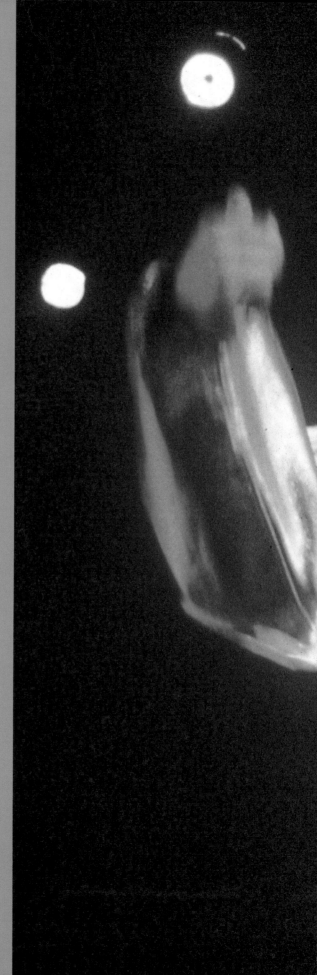

K E I T H   D U F F Y

KEITH BOUNDS OFF THE TOUR BUS, FLASHING A SMILE FROM EAR TO EAR AT THE GAGGLE OF FANS WHO'VE SURROUNDED THE VEHICLE. TOWERING OVER THE GIRLS WITH HIS LARGE FRAME, HE LOOKS MORE LIKE A MEMBER OF THE SECURITY TEAM.

Fans are often afraid to approach him because of his imposing stature. "For a while, I had a skin-head haircut, that really frightened them off," he laughs later when I mention this to him. Keith may have the appearance of a hard man, but his features hide a sensitive, caring nature. "How'yas," he exclaims as the fans press forward to touch their idols. "Hope yez enjoy the show."

On tour, Keith, like the other members of the group, is always willing to sign autographs and pose for photographs with the fans who come up to him.

His whole face glows with a mixture of pride and joy as the girls chatter excitedly among themselves after securing the personal signatures of the Boyz.

"Ah, it's a good feeling," Keith reveals as he prepares for a sound check. "It's the best feeling in the world, experiencing that kind of love and devotion. It's a tremendous boost to the ego."

With his striking good looks, strong physique and cheeky personality, you would assume that Keith Duffy never lacked confidence when he hit his teenage years and discovered the attractions of the opposite

"I'M PROBABLY CONSIDERED THE MOUTH IN THE GROUP NOW. BUT I THINK THE LADS RESPECT ME FOR THAT. I SAY WHAT THEY'RE THINKING."

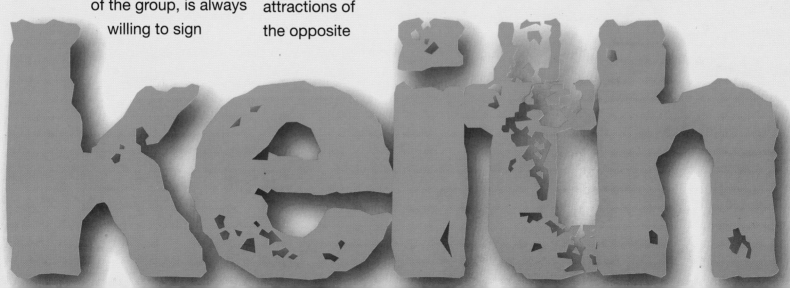

sex. But he had the same insecurities as everyone else coming to terms with adolescence.

"I fancied loads of girls, but I never had the confidence to approach them. Even if I was told that the girl I fancied, fancied me back, I'd never go and talk to her for fear of rejection. I was always afraid that they wouldn't like the person behind the front, if you know what I mean.

"As a result of that, girls thought I was just being big headed and snobbish...that I felt I was too good for them. They started calling me 'poser', 'big head' and 'shaper' and, basically, everybody thought I loved myself too much to even go out with girls.

"The reality is, deep down I was insecure. I would have loved to have gone out with them, but I didn't have the confidence in myself. Keith has had to grow up very fast, not only because of the

"AT WEEKENDS, MY MATES WOULD BE OFF WITH THEIR GIRLS AND I WAS LEFT ON MY OWN. FOR A LONG TIME I WAS CRYING OUT FOR A RELATIONSHIP."

responsibilities that Boyzone has imposed on him, but also because he's now a DAD.

On tour, Keith spends a lot of time on the phone, making sure that his girlfriend Lisa is aware of his love and support for her and the baby.

While Boyzone has played a major role in shaping the 'new man' that is Keith Duffy, his girlfriend has also been a major influence on his life.

"I had a solid relationship with Lisa before the band ever achieved fame. She stayed with me through thick and thin. She supported me for a long time when I had no money. I've grown up with her.

"She's nearly five years older than me and she had it all together when I still didn't have a clue. She helped me build my character, build my confidence

**"I never grew up with girls because there are all boys in my family, so I didn't have much interaction with** girls

Now I have a lot of friends in this business

who are girls and I don't have any hang-ups

about myself. I'm not shy anymore."

I love her, y'know."
Dressed in a pair of shorts and sweat-soaked T-shirt, Keith heads for a shower in his hotel room. As he straddles the divide between his personal life and his career, the star occasionally reaches boiling point. His physical workouts in the gym help to defuse some of the stress that builds up.

"From time to time, the loneliness and pain does kick in, but I have to be strong for myself and my family and do the business."

Keith is the voice of the band. During business meetings, he's the one who pipes up if there are questions to be answered or items to be clarified. He may be the joker in the pack, as you'll read elsewhere about his activities, but he takes a serious approach to affairs that may affect the individuals in the group.

If Boyzone have an axe to grind or if they feel that they're being pushed past their limits, it's Keith who'll say what has to be said to the top brass.

"I went through a stage last year where I got very depressed because we were doing so much. It was endless promotion, endless interviews, endless photo sessions, endless travelling and I began to pile on the weight.

and turn me into the person I am today.

"For me to turn around now and have a fling or leap into an affair with another girl, that would be taking advantage of what she's done for me over the years. It would be like saying, 'Thanks very much for that, I don't need you now, I'm running off with someone else,' and that's not the type of bloke I am. And that's not to say I'm staying with her because I owe her, I'm staying with her because

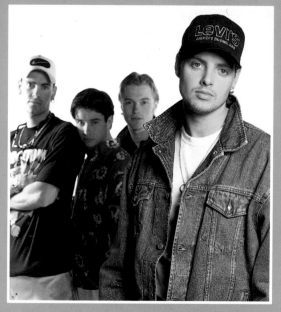

"It was getting me down. We had no time for a proper life. Eventually I just said, 'ENOUGH.' We need our time

"MY MOTHER'S REALLY PROUD OF WHAT

I'VE ACHIEVED THROUGH BOYZONE AND

WHAT I'VE DONE WITH MY LIFE. BUT

SOMEHOW I SUSPECT THAT SHE STILL

REGARDS ME AS HER LITTLE BOY."

# "It's very hard to leave a

off. We're human beings. We're not machines. Life is not worth this."

It's seldom a day will pass that Keith doesn't have a conversation with his mum, Pat, back home in Dublin. Even though he's the second eldest, there's a special relationship between Pat and Keith. And it has nothing to do with the fact that he has achieved notoriety as a pop star.

"When I was about four years old, I had pneumonia and whooping cough and a load of other things and I was in hospital for a year. My mother came to live in the hospital with me and we kind of created a bond between each other. She loves my two brothers just as much as she loves me, but we have a special bond."

While Keith obviously revels in his role as a showbiz personality, there are times when the attention of the media turns sour.

Going through the airport with Lisa and their baby son Jordan, shortly after they became parents, they were confronted by a tenacious newspaper photographer.

Keith freaked out as the snapper tried desperately to get the first exclusive close up of the baby.

He lunged at the guy and it was only the intervention of Shane that saved

# little child behind and go off on tour. When the baby came along it was a very, very emotional time for me.

Keith from a possible assault charge. Later, when he'd cooled down, Keith explained: "I don't mind that kind of attention.

The loss of privacy is part of our business.

"But when I'm not working and I'm with my family, I'm very sensitive to the effect it's having on them."

# It's the most amazing thing that has ever happened to me in my life."

"THERE WAS A TIME WHEN I'D LET PEOPLE WALK ALL OVER ME BECAUSE I WANTED TO BE PERCEIVED AS THE EASY-GOING, GAME FOR A LAUGH, FRIENDLY BLOKE THAT EVERYONE LOVES. BUT IN THIS GAME YOU HAVE TO TOUGHEN UP. BOYZONE IS MY JOB AND MY JOB INVOLVES BEING AWAY A LOT. IT HASN'T BEEN EASY. IF I DIDN'T BLOCK OUT SOME OF MY FEELINGS I WOULDN'T BE ABLE TO DO IT AT ALL."

"IT'S BEEN A TOUGH COUPLE OF YEARS FOR ME.

I"M THRILLED WITH THE SUCCESS OF BOYZONE

BUT IT HAS BROUGHT A LOT OF PRESSURE TOO."

MIKEY PONDERS THE FUTURE, THINKS LONG AND HARD, THEN IS QUITE ADAMANT WHEN HE SAYS THAT BOYZONE WILL NEVER SPLIT LIKE TAKE THAT.

"At the end of the day, no matter who we have around us, whether it's our management or the record company, the core is the five of us and we have to look after each other."

Closeness is the key to their lives. And if the strong bond holds between the Famous Five then it will power them on to even greater achievements.

They're a group with huge potential that hasn't been fully tapped. There is no doubt that they have many more surprises up their sleeves as their career continues to expand beyond everyone's expectations.

Success generates wealth and it will allow them to produce even more spectacular live shows that are already being planned for the future.

Mikey says: "Up to now we've been concentrating on the dancing and the singing. Now we want to move on and look at how we can develop the show in other areas. We want to be the

**"WE'RE MUCH CLOSER AS A GROUP THAN TAKE THAT. IF ONE OF US HAD A PROBLEM LIKE ROBBIE WILLIAMS, THE OTHER FOUR WOULD BE THERE TO HELP HIM OUT."**

**"IF ONE OF US HAS A FALL, THE OTHERS PICK HIM BACK UP. IT'S ALL ABOUT TOGETHERNESS."**

best... the best that we can be."

Ronan adds: "It's new challenges that keep the adrenalin pumping. Going to new places and winning over people who're seeing us for the first time, that's the buzz.

"Getting people excited is what it's all about. That's what we get off on. That's what keeps us fresh and eager. Eager to please. That's us."

It's a couple of hours before a Boyzone concert and two delirious young fans are escorted into the inner sanctum of the Boyz' camp, pinching themselves because they can't believe their good fortune.

They have just realised every young girl's dream of getting up close to their favourite pop stars.

Ronan, Steve, Shane, Mikey and Keith pose for souvenir pics and sign their autographs.

Then the luckiest girls on earth are taken into the bowels of the building where they're granted a private audience with pin-up hunks Ronan and Shane in their dressing-room.

The mesmerised pair, Catherine and Yvonne, had their prayers answered when they won a competition to interview the Boyz.

Nervously flicking open her list of questions, Catherine asks: What is the strangest thing a fan has ever done to you?

**Ronan:** I don't know. There's a lot of things the fans do for us. They send us crazy things in the post. But there's nothing I can pick out. The fans are great. If it wasn't for them, we wouldn't be where we are.

**Yvonne:** What qualities do you look for in a girl?

**Shane:** Well, because we have been around the world so many times and seen so many different kinds of people, we don't actually have one quality that we look for in girls... other than to be themselves. I don't particularly look for girls who are blonde or have brown eyes or blue eyes or whatever. What comes, comes. You fall in love, you fall in love.

**Catherine:** How do you keep in shape?

**Shane:** Every night, Ronan and I always do our push-ups. Even if we've been to the bar!

**Catherine:** Who's the wildest member of the band?

**Shane:** Probably the loudest, rather than the wildest, would be Keith. He's the loudest. He's the troublemaker. Wherever there's trouble he's in the middle of it. If something is broken, he did it. If anyone is fighting, he's always in it.

**Yvonne:** Who gets the most fan mail?

**Shane:** Steve, definitely. But we all get our fair share.

**Catherine:** Ronan, being the youngest member of the group, do you think you have the right to be mature?

**Ronan:** Everybody has the right to do what they like. That's a weird question. I am what I am. I don't try to be anything I'm not.

**Yvonne:** What would you be doing now if you hadn't become part of Boyzone.

**Shane:** I'd be a mechanic. I'd be working for my Da in his garage. Getting my hands dirty and all that.

**Catherine:** Will you ever let fame go to your head?

**Shane:** You couldn't do that. Then it would be no fun.

**Ronan:** No, we try our best to keep our feet on the ground. Keep ourselves sane.

**Shane:** It hasn't gone to our heads. We still slag each other.

**Catherine:** Would you ever have a serious relationship with one of your fans?

**Shane:** I don't know. It all depends if I fell in love with someone.

Then Shane, noticing a scar over Catherine's eye, asks: Now, I have a question. What happened to your eyebrow?

**Catherine:** I hit it on a metal bar at our local football club.

**Shane:** I'm jealous because that's a real scar and this (pointing to his shaved eyebrow) is not.

Then all too soon for the girls, they're whisked away. Outside in the arena the fans are anxiously waiting for the Boyz to appear on stage. Waiting to be taken up to heaven as Boyzone weave their magic.

## ACKNOWLEDGMENTS

A heartfelt Thank You to my family, friends and colleagues for their support during the work on this book. In particular, a special thank you to my friend Louis Walsh, the manager of Boyzone, who offered me the chance to capture a piece of Irish pop history with this book. To his partner John Reynolds and to five great guys for their faith in me: Ronan, Keith, Steve, Mikey and Shane. Thanks Boyz.

To Colm MacGinty, Editor of my newspaper, the Sunday World, for his support and encouragement. And to my Sunday World colleagues Sean Boyne (The Guru), Val Sheehan (The Photographer) and Sarah Hamilton (The Cuttings Supremo) for all their help.

To Paul Keogh of Polygram, the man who signed up the biggest pop group to come out of Ireland; to his team working on Boyzone, including Ailish Toohey and Sharon Dunne. To Carol Hanna of Carol & Associates and Lynne Fitzgerald of Brookham PR. And to Philip Dodd, the publisher, and all at Virgin Publishing in London.

Most of all, to my wonderful wife, Patricia, and daughters Kate, who is aged four and madly in love with Ronan, and baby Laura.

## PICTURE CREDITS

**All photographs supplied by Idols Licensing & Publicity Ltd © Idols Licensing & Publicity Ltd**

**Ray Burmiston**: front cover, flaps, 1, 3, 5, 6, 8, 11 both photos, 16, 17, 18, 19, 20, 21 all photos, 22 all photos, 23, 24-25, 25, 26, 31 bottom, 33, 35, 36, 37, 38 all photos, 39, 40 all photos, 41, 42, 45, 46 right, 48 top, 51 inset, 54, 56 all photos, 57, 58, 59 both photos, 60 all photos, 61, 62-63, 63, 64, 66, 67, 68, 69 top right and middle, 73, 74, 75, 76 all photos, 77, 78, both photos, 79, 80-81, 82, 86 top left and bottom right, 91, 93, 94, 94-95, 96;

**Fabio Nosotti**: 32 top right, 70 top;

**Mike Prior**: 53, 72, 89;

**Tim Roney**: back cover, 10, 12, 13 all photos, 27, 28, 29, 32 top left, middle, bottom left and right, 34-35, 46 left, 47, 48 bottom right, 49, 51 background, 69 bottom left, 70 bottom right, 71, 84, 85 both photos, 86 middle, 87, 88, 90, 92;

**Dave Willis**: 14, 15, 30, 31 top, 48 bottom left, 52-53, 70 middle and bottom left.

**OFFICIAL BOYZONE MERCHANDISE** available from Underworld, PO Box 7575, London E1 9GN